KING GEORGE III ISSUED FOOD STAM[P]

GOLFERS DRIVE CADDIES

ANTIQUE CARS HAVE CRANKY MOTORS

DARWIN WAS A MONKEY'S UNC[LE]

DR. FRANKENSTEIN DID BODY WOR[K]

THE PENTAGON HAS A SERVICE ENTRANCE

Q's ARE WEIRD O's

MUFFLERS ARE A SOUND INVESTMEN[T]

CHRISTMAS STOCKINGS HAVE THEIR HANG-UPS

CAMELOT WAS FAMOUS FOR ITS KNIGHT LIFE

HORSE OPERAS ARE BANG TALES

ABIES WEAR SEEP-THROUGH CLOTHES

OHNSONS WAX HATES POLISH JOKES

NORTH TEXANS ARE PANHANDLERS

NDERELLA, PLEASE DON'T SQUEEZE THE CHARMING

OAH EBSTER AD SPELLS

THE FLUE GETS SANTA CLAUS DOWN

HORATIO WAS A BRIDGE EXPERT

WHAT'S HIS NAME IS THE FORGOTTEN MAN

ILLARD LMORE IS NOT A DUCK

Q'S ARE WEIRD O'S:

More Puns, Gags, Quips and Riddles

Roy Doty

What kind of cow goes "Beeeeeeeeep Beeeeeeeeeep"?

What resembles a large blob and has chrome stripes?

What kind of plant eats a ton of meat all at once?

What was Count Dracula doing at the baseball stadium?

MILLARD FILLMORE PUN, GAG, QUIP & RIDDLE CLUB

Doty

DOUBLEDAY & COMPANY   GARDEN CITY, NEW YORK

Library of Congress Cataloging in Publication Data

Doty, Roy, 1922–
    Q's are weird O's.

        1.   Riddles—Juvenile literature.   2.   Wit and humor,
Juvenile.   I.   Title.
ISBN 0-385-02403-7 TRADE
        0-385-02404-5 PREBOUND
PN6371.5.D6   793.7'35

Library of Congress Catalog Card Number 74-17379

KING GEORGE III ISSUED FOOD STAM[PS]

GOLFERS DRIVE CADDIES

ANTIQUE CARS
HAVE CRANKY MOTORS

DARWIN
WAS A
MONKEY'S UNC[LE]

DR. FRANKENSTEIN DID BODY WOR[K]

THE PENTAGON
HAS A
SERVICE ENTRANCE

Q's ARE
WEIRD O's

MUFFLERS ARE A SOUND INVESTMEN[T]

CHRISTMAS STOCKINGS
HAVE THEIR HANG-UPS

CAMELOT WAS FAMOUS FOR
ITS KNIGHT LIFE

HORSE OPERAS ARE BANG TALES

BIES WEAR SEEP-THROUGH CLOTHES

OHNSONS WAX
HATES
OLISH JOKES

NORTH TEXANS ARE
PANHANDLERS

DERELLA, PLEASE DON'T SQUEEZE
THE CHARMING

OAH
BSTER
D SPELLS

THE FLUE GETS
SANTA CLAUS DOWN

HORATIO WAS A
BRIDGE EXPERT

WHAT'S HIS NAME
IS THE
ORGOTTEN MAN

LLARD
LMORE
S NOT A
DUCK

Date Due

DEC 1 1975		
DEC 5 1975		
DEC 19 1975		
APR 21 1977 Keefe		
NOV 11 1977		
APR 19 1978 Newman		
APR 20 1978		
DEC 1 1978		
Garcia		
DEC 19		
NOV 9 1988		
FEB 28 1988		
OCT 9 1992		

Demco 38-297